BEAUTY OF
THE FATHER

BY NILO CRUZ

★

★

DRAMATISTS
PLAY SERVICE
INC.

*For Maria Angeles Sanz, who opened the doors
to her house and let me stay in the town of
Salobreña, Granada. And to the memory of
Federico García Lorca, who had housed me long ago
in Granada, through his plays and his poetry.*

BEAUTY OF THE FATHER received its world premiere by the New Theatre (Rafael de Acha, Artistic Director; Eileen Suarez, Managing Director) in Coral Gables, Florida, on January 3, 2004. It was directed by Rafael De Acha; the set design was by Adrian W. Jones; the lighting design was by Travis Neff; the sound design was by Ozzie Quintana; and the costume and props design were by Caron Grant. The cast was as follows:

MARINA .... Ursula Freundlich
EMILIANO .... Roberto Escobar
PAQUITA .... Teresa Maria Rojas
KARIM .... Euriamis Losada
FEDERICO GARCÍA LORCA .... Carlos Orizondo

BEAUTY OF THE FATHER received its New York City premiere by Manhattan Theatre Club (Lynne Meadow, Artistic Director; Barry Grove, Executive Producer) on December 8, 2005. It was directed by Michael Greif; the set design was by Mark Wendland; the costume design was by Miranda Hoffman; the lighting design was by James F. Ingalls; the sound design was by Darron L. West; the general manager was Florie Seery; the production stage manager was Barclay Stiff; the stage manager was David H. Lurie; the production manager was Ryan McMahon; and the fight direction was by Rick Sordelet. The cast was as follows:

MARINA .... Elizabeth Rodriguez
EMILIANO .... Ritchie Coster
PAQUITA .... Priscilla Lopez
KARIM .... Pedro Pascal
FEDERICO GARCÍA LORCA .... Oscar Isaac

CHARACTERS

MARINA — a young woman of twenty-five

EMILIANO — a man in his mid-forties, early fifties

PAQUITA — a woman in her late-forties, early fifties

KARIM — a young man of twenty-five

FEDERICO GARCÍA LORCA — the thirty-eight-year-old poet as a ghost, dressed in a white suit

PLACE

The action of the play takes place in a small town called Salobreña, in Granada, Spain.

TIME

Summer of 1998.

SET

The open terrace of an old Spanish beach house that faces the Mediterranean. The terrace has been converted into a sort of artist studio because of its open space and view of the sea. There are wooden sculptures, canvases and a rifle hangs from a wall. The furniture and decoration have a Moroccan influence.

Note: The character of Lorca always does a simple turn to make himself invisible.

"The sky has shores where life can be avoided
And there are bodies that shouldn't repeat themselves at dawn."

—*Federico García Lorca*

BEAUTY OF THE FATHER

ACT ONE

Scene 1

The sound of bells. A long shaft of orange light bathes Federico García Lorca. He is dressed in a 1930s white linen suit.

LORCA. Five o'clock in the afternoon. The hour that bullfighters get killed. *(Writes a note.)*

There was no death today at five o'clock in the afternoon. No, no death reported. Perhaps there was a wound. But there is always a wound in the world, open and exposed for everybody to see, and a little sand bucket of tears by the edge of the sea. *(A flash of white light. Emiliano stands with a pair of espadrilles in the palms of his hands. Flamenco music plays.)*

EMILIANO. This is a picture of a pair of espadrilles I bought for you.

In the South of Spain we use espadrilles in the summer.

If you come to Salobreña, you have a pair waiting for you.

Now that your mother is no longer alive, why don't you come and live with me.

Love your father, Emiliano. *(A flash of white light. Marina stands holding an old birdcage.)*

MARINA. This is a picture of me with a birdcage I bought at the market.

I'm going to buy myself a green parakeet.

This way the house will seem less lonely.

I can't get used to living without Mamá.

I think I'm coming to see you. *(Marina exits. A flash of white light. Emiliano holds a bird's nest.)*

EMILIANO. This is a picture of a nest I found in one of my walks to the woods.

I've been making sculptures of nests ever since you told me that you're coming to see me.

I want to father you again after all these years.

Don't buy the green parakeet. Just come to Spain! *(A flash of white light.)*

LORCA. I would've been a hundred this year. Yes, me, Federico García Lorca. But now I'm dead and gone, and there is no difference between a wisp of smoke and myself, so I constantly have to remind myself that I'm only a spirit and I have to look at life from a distance and not get too involved with humanity. But the living have a way of beckoning us back to life through prayer or a work of art, and sometimes what pulls us to the world exists independently of our will. And it's only natural that we respond, because as spirits we have our little sad attachments to the world, and there's always work to be done. *(The lights change. Paquita enters the stage running. She holds a cloth and is drying her hands.)*

PAQUITA. She's here, Emiliano. She called from the airport. She took an earlier flight from Madrid.

EMILIANO. How long ago did she call?

PAQUITA. Twenty minutes.

EMILIANO. How do I look? Why didn't you call me?

PAQUITA. I did. But your phone didn't pick up.

EMILIANO. Where are my car keys? I have to change my shirt.

PAQUITA. No. You stay here. I sent Karim to pick her up in your car.

EMILIANO. Will he recognize her? He doesn't know her.

PAQUITA. *Vale, hombre! Calmate!* Calm down ... He's seen pictures of her.

EMILIANO. Damn it! I wanted to pick her up at the airport. *(He takes out his cellular phone.)* What's wrong with this shit!

PAQUITA. I'll go tell Tomasa she can start preparing lunch. *(Paquita exits. Emiliano stays alone with Lorca.)*

EMILIANO. It's my daughter.

LORCA. Good!

EMILIANO. I have to pick up this place. I started painting and I made a mess ... *(In a sort of frenzy he starts organizing the mess on top of his worktable.)*

LORCA. How long has it been since you saw her last?

EMILIANO. Almost ten years.

LORCA. Why that long?

EMILIANO. Her mother thought I was unfit as a father.

LORCA. And what on earth does that mean?

EMILIANO. I think you understand.

LORCA. Bah, that's like saying that a woman in order to be a mother has to knit, milk cows and know how to cut a sausage.

EMILIANO. I have to change my shirt.

LORCA. Then change your shirt, *hombre,* and wash your face. You've been out in the fields gathering your nests. You must smell like a horse. *(Emiliano runs offstage to get a clean shirt.)*

EMILIANO. Yes, I want to look good. I don't want her to get the wrong impression of her father. *(He enters wearing a clean shirt.)* We really don't know each other that well. I left home when she was a little girl. Does this shirt look better?

LORCA. Much better. Oh, I wish I had a daughter! *(Emiliano sees a mess under the table and starts arranging his paint tubes.)*

EMILIANO. I have to pick up these paints. And if you don't mind, Federico, I don't think you should be around when she gets here.

LORCA. Ashamed to introduce me?

EMILIANO. No. But what would she think when she sees that I converse with a dead man?

LORCA. Thank you, my dear. Perhaps I should leave now.

EMILIANO. No, I didn't mean ... Not just a dead man, my dear friend Federico García Lorca —

Did you have anything to do with my daughter coming?

LORCA. Do you think I can perform miracles?

EMILIANO. I don't know. You're the first dead man I've met —

LORCA. Departed, Emiliano. Perished. There are words that can alleviate reality. *(Paquita enters running.)*

PAQUITA. The car just pulled in. They're taking the bags out of the trunk. Oh, she's even more beautiful than the photos. And she speaks Spanish, too!

EMILIANO. How do I look?

PAQUITA. You look fine! You look fine! Let's go! Let's go! *(She starts to go, then stops.)* Oh wait! So what are we going to tell your daughter when she asks about me?

EMILIANO. *(Playfully.)* We'll tell her that you had a lobotomy and forgot who you are!

PAQUITA. You fool! *(Hits him playfully.)*

EMILIANO. Let's go! Let's go! *(Paquita and Emiliano start to exit. Emiliano signals Lorca to leave.)*

LORCA. A whole new life is starting for you, Emiliano. A new beginning.

Now you'll recover your place in the world and you'll cease to be an exiled father. Just remember that your past with your daughter never made it to the future, so you might encounter that unforeseen tear. *(Lorca exits. We hear laughter outside. Marina, Emiliano, Paquita and Karim enter the stage.)*

MARINA. *(Entering.)* You should've seen what happened, Papá. Should I tell him? *(Breaks into laughter.)*

EMILIANO. Don't tell me he was late to the station.

KARIM. She makes me laugh.

MARINA. I won't tell you if you're going to get upset with him.

EMILIANO. No. I don't think anything can make me upset today. *(Changes tone.)* So what did you do, Karim?

KARIM. *(Looks at her and breaks into laughter.)* Your daughter makes me laugh.

MARINA. We got into a little accident.

EMILIANO. Oh! That can make me upset.

PAQUITA. *Vale hombre!* Let them explain.

MARINA. It wasn't his fault, Papá.

EMILIANO. What's a little accident, Karim?

KARIM. *(Looks at her and begins to laugh again.)* I can't look at her ...

MARINA. He was taking a curve and all of a sudden there was a deer crossing the road. He tried to steer the car away and the wheels started to skid and the car went around in circles.

PAQUITA. Did you hurt yourself?

MARINA. No, no, we're fine. It was like being in a roller coaster, right? *(Karim does a circle with his hand.)*

KARIM. *(Laughs.)* Isn't she funny! Isn't she beautiful!

EMILIANO. Was he playing his loud music? *(Looks at Karim. Karim looks at her and breaks into laughter again.)*

MARINA. *(She laughs with him.)* I was the one who told him to play it loud. Being around all those mountains, it felt like there was so much freedom all around us, so much room to breathe and take in life.

I told him to step on the accelerator and to blast up the music!

KARIM. You see, she's lovely! You have a beautiful daughter.

MARINA. I think it's the only time I have felt like myself since Mamá died.

EMILIANO. Well, you are here now and that's what matters.

PAQUITA. So, did anything happen to the deer?

KARIM. Oh no! We saved his life.

PAQUITA. Then nothing really happened. Nothing happened to Marina. Nothing happened to you. Nothing happened to the deer. We don't have anything to worry about. Let's have café! Welcome to Spain, Marina! Welcome to Salobreña!

EMILIANO. What about my car?

PAQUITA. Ah, hombre! Nothing happened to the car! *(Starts to make her way to the kitchen.)* Let's drink café. Marina, please don't tell me that you don't drink café.

MARINA. I do.

PAQUITA. Good. You have our same sweet habits. I hope you smoke, too.

MARINA. No, I don't.

PAQUITA. Ah, don't worry. I'll smoke on your behalf. *(Paquita and Karim exit.)*

MARINA. Are they for real?

EMILIANO. After you've had six glasses of wine, yes.

MARINA. I like them.

EMILIANO. Good!

MARINA. So you're not as lonely as I thought you'd be.

EMILIANO. No. I've become a nester. I've created a family for myself, and now with you here the family is complete.

MARINA. I did buy a roundtrip ticket —

EMILIANO. Good. They're cheaper.

MARINA. No. I mean —

EMILIANO. So don't use it —

MARINA. What about my university — ?

EMILIANO. We have universities here —

MARINA. I just —

EMILIANO. Relax. Breathe. At least let me try to convince you to stay.

MARINA. I'm sure I'll be tempted. *(She looks around. Emiliano signals.)* It's a beautiful house, and so close to the sea. Do you always get this breeze?

EMILIANO. Always. *(He looks at her full of love.)* Come here. Let me look at you. *(Marina walks to another part of the stage. We can sense that she doesn't feel quite comfortable with her father.)*

MARINA. Oh, I probably look like a scarecrow. I didn't sleep a bit on the airplane. I'm exhausted. Since Mamá's death I haven't stopped working. I had to take care of so many things. I don't think

13

I've ever worked so hard in my life.

EMILIANO. Why did you take so long to tell me about your mother's death?

MARINA. I promised her not to tell you. She told me to wait a while.

EMILIANO. Is that because — ?

MARINA. She didn't want you at the funeral.

EMILIANO. Why?

MARINA. She didn't want you to see her helpless and dead.

EMILIANO. Did she let Robert go to her funeral?

MARINA. Why wouldn't she? He was her husband. *(Emiliano walks to another part of the room confused.)*

EMILIANO. I always think it's terrible these things …

MARINA. Just see it as another way of loving. Is this what you are painting now? *(Lorca enters.)*

EMILIANO. Yes, all these. Do you know Lorca?

MARINA. Mama had all his books. She always said if you ever want to know about your father read his work. *(Lorca laughs.)*

EMILIANO. And did you?

MARINA. Yes. *(Marina glances everywhere. She moves close to the table where Emiliano keeps a few nests.)*

MARINA. Are these the nests that you found?

EMILIANO. Yes.

MARINA. *(Marina picks up one of the nests.)* Don't you feel bad about taking them?

EMILIANO. No. They've been abandoned.

MARINA. But they say that birds always come back to their nests.

EMILIANO. I always ask for permission before I take them. I have manners. They're the ones that are rude. They nest on my roof without asking me.

MARINA. Are these the espadrilles? *(Karim enters.)*

KARIM. Paquita wants you out on the patio. She's serving café there.

EMILIANO. Tell her we'll be there in a second. *(Karim exits.)*

MARINA. Why the sculptures of nests?

EMILIANO. Because I knew you were coming, because I'd like to father you.

MARINA. I'm not a child anymore.

EMILIANO. You are my child no matter how old you are. Let's go. *(He places his hand on her shoulder with affection.)* You and I are starting from scratch. You are Marina and I am Emiliano, and

14

we've been brought together by life once again. Let's have café. Your first café in Spain.

LORCA. That's it, my friend! You're handling it well. Later you have to show her the sea. Let her know that this is where Spain ends and rocks spill over the edge to welcome those who come with pain and affliction. *(Flamenco music plays. Lights change.)*

Scene 2

Emiliano stands next to a painting he is making of Lorca. He is cleaning his paintbrushes with a rag and is passionately involved in conversation. Lorca is sitting in a chair.

EMILIANO. I mean these were men who left everything back home just to come here and fight in the Spanish Civil War! My father was one of those men. He bought himself a uniform at the army-navy surplus. He disguised himself as a tourist and left on a ship. Then when he got to France he took a train to a town close to the Pyrenees, and there he joined the international troops. And can you believe these men fought this war as if they were fighting for their own land? And some never made it back alive. My own father lost his right leg in this war. But the good thing is when he went back home he brought with him a wife, who later became my mother. And up until the end he always joked about his missing leg by saying, "Wherever I stand I'll always have one leg in Spain." *(Laughs.)* — Come with me and I'll show you how this is coming along. Close ... OK ... *(He shows him the canvas.)* Now this part is unfinished and this part is lacking the final touch. But you can more or less have a sense of the whole composition.

LORCA. It's wonderful.

EMILIANO. It's getting there.

LORCA. No. It's amazing. Little by little you define rough edges and shape my body. My bones. My skin. My clavicle. The neck that once held my head. Look at that! *(Points to the painting.)* Little by little you're rescuing me from the mud — from the soil — from the maggots — from the ants — from the other bodies that were thrown in the pit. The bullets are coming out my body. The black crows. The smell of gunpowder. The punch of death. It's all here in this painting. But, nobody wants to talk about these things. Nobody wants to talk about the dead.

EMILIANO. Nobody could talk about it when Franco was in power. But now Spain has changed and all the graves should be found and the victims should be identified and buried properly.

LORCA. That's a lot of bones to dig out. I was killed like a dog, like an animal. And all because I was a poet and I had my own ideas in life. "Kill the faggot," they said. "Kill the communist and leave his eyes wide open so he can see why he was killed." Do you know that when a man is buried with open eyes he can never find rest? Do you know that I am attentive like that child who sits in the first row of a classroom wanting to grasp a lesson, except I don't know what I am supposed to learn? One thing for certain, I'm always cold. There's always a northern wind all around me. A chill. And I'm from here — the south. Heat. Sunflowers. Gypsies.

MARINA. *(From offstage.)* Papá!

EMILIANO. *(In a loud voice.)* Yes.

MARINA. *(Offstage.)* Whose hats are these inside the blue box?

EMILIANO. *(In a loud voice.)* They belonged to the lady who used to live here.

MARINA. *(Offstage.)* And what's inside the white box?

EMILIANO. *(In a loud voice.)* That's mine. Don't open that one. Don't be offended, Federico, but come back later, will you? *(Emiliano hears his daughter approaching.)*

LORCA. Oh, for God's sake! Are we going to go through this again? I can always make myself invisible, my friend.

EMILIANO. Go now! *(The door opens. Marina enters wearing a hat and holding a box. Lorca stays in the room watching. Emiliano becomes uneasy with Lorca's presence.)*

MARINA. How do I look? Can I wear it?

LORCA. Marvelous. Wear it.

EMILIANO. *(Dissimulating Lorca's presence.)* Sure. Marvelous. Wear it.

MARINA. I like this one the best. But I also like this other one for spring, and this one for the beach. Mamá used to say that there's a whole language to hats. There are hats for every occasion and mood. *(She tries on another hat. Lorca starts trying on some of the hats she places back on the box.)* I guess this one would be for melancholy.

LORCA. No. We don't want melancholy.

EMILIANO. No melancholy.

MARINA. Hats that make you mysterious.

EMILIANO. Now that's mysterious.

MARINA. Yes, to visit the Alhambra palace on a rainy day. Tell me if you like this one for a rendezvous.

EMILIANO. Did you meet somebody already? You just got here.

MARINA. No, but I'd like to fall in love in Granada.

LORCA. Wear the first one.

EMILIANO. *(Dissimulating.)* I like the first one. *(Marina tries on another hat.)*

LORCA. She's quite a darling, Emiliano!

MARINA. Ah, Mamá had a hat like this one. It's lovely, isn't it?

EMILIANO. Yes, it is.

MARINA. She looked so beautiful the day she died. No one would think … She died with such grace. That afternoon she said, "Pass me my purse. Let me look at my face in the mirror." She opened her compact, looked at herself and said, "Oh, I look fine." Then she asked me to play music. She said she only wanted to hear Fados. And I played her Amalia Rodrigues. All of a sudden her face became vibrant, as if she had reached into her purse and pulled out her last strand of life. She got up and asked me to dance with her. "Listen to that voice," she'd repeat over and over again. "Listen to the clarity of that voice." Then she sat in her chair and she took her last breath listening to Amalia's voice.

And I was actually proud of myself that day. I didn't get hysterical or anything. I didn't call the doctor or the rescue right away. Instead, I took my time before she was taken away from me. I let the music play on. I combed her hair and powdered her face.

I colored her lips and perfumed her neck. And I sat there and looked at her as if she were a painting, because I tell you, Papá, she looked like a masterpiece of life that was. And when the rescue came, they wanted to know at what time this, at what time that. And I wasn't much help. I told them she had just come back from a dance — that my mother had just come back from Spain after dancing with my father. *(Laughs.)* They must've thought I was mad.

EMILIANO. Come on! Don't get sad. *(Paquita enters.)*

PAQUITA. Ah, you're still up! I fell asleep in the patio looking at the night. There are so many stars out this evening. I saw about three shooting stars.

MARINA. Did you make a wish?

PAQUITA. I did. Three wishes. And tomorrow I'm playing bingo and buying a lottery ticket. Good night!

17

EMILIANO. Sleep well!

MARINA. I'm going to bed too. *(Marina kisses her father.)*

EMILIANO. Sleep well, my child. *(Marina exits. Emiliano looks at Lorca.)* Did you hear what she said?

LORCA. Of course I did.

EMILIANO. Dancing with me! *(Karim enters with a rifle.)*

KARIM. *Hola!* You're still up? Has everybody gone to bed?

EMILIANO. Yes. What are you doing with that rifle?

KARIM. I'm going to kill the fox that's been circling the house. He tried getting inside the cage where I keep the rabbits, and since he couldn't get in, he went under the cage and started biting and eating the paws of the rabbits. When I woke up in the morning I found four dead rabbits without paws. They had bled to death.

EMILIANO. And are you going to stay up all night?

KARIM. No. I should be going to bed. The fox should be making his way back here soon. Once a fox knows where there's food he comes back for more. Yesterday, I set up a trap. I left one of the dead rabbits next to the stable, and every hour I checked to see if the fox had come back to eat. At around ten thirty the dead rabbit was gone. That means the fox had its meal around this time, and tonight he'll be making his way back again. Except, I'll be there to surprise him. *(Emiliano moves closer to Karim.)*

EMILIANO. So what are you going to do after you do your killing?

KARIM. Wash my hands and go to sleep.

EMILIANO. *(With seduction.)* And why don't you come to my room and surprise me? Why don't you have a drink with me?

KARIM. Emiliano, come on …

EMILIANO. *(Touches his face.)* Why not?

KARIM. *(He pulls his hand away.)* I told you last time …

EMILIANO. *(Touches his shoulder.)* You told me what?

KARIM. Oh, come on! Your daughter is here.

EMILIANO. *(Touches his neck.)* So?

KARIM. *(Moves away from him.)* I told you I didn't want —

EMILIANO. *(Grabs his arm.)* You like my daughter, don't you?

KARIM. No.

EMILIANO. I know you do.

KARIM. Come on … Stop it! *(Moves away from him.)*

EMILIANO. I'll wait for you in my room. *(Karim looks at him, then exits.)*

LORCA. This boy Karim will be the end of you.

EMILIANO. Why do you say that? *(Emiliano goes for a drink.)*

LORCA. I can see.

EMILIANO. He's been difficult sometimes. But I knew this from the beginning; from the moment I picked him off the streets.

LORCA. And why do you persist?

EMILIANO. Because I'm a romantic fool, and I can't let go of him!

LORCA. I was a fool like you. I don't remember ever finding love in life.

Faces and the form of human bodies, that's all I ever found.

Love has always been a thick forest that I've never been able to enter, and all I've known is the promise of the trees. The cry of an animal trapped in a zoo, aiming for the color green. *(Sound of a shotgun. Lorca jumps up as if remembering the day he was shot and then he shakes off the fright. Emiliano stares at Lorca.)* Ha! The boy must have shot the fox. *(Moroccan music plays.)*

Scene 3

Karim is sitting on the floor. He has several small bottles of oils and perfumes on top of an arabesque cloth. He's using a dropper to measure the perfume he's transferring from one bottle to another. Marina enters drying her hair.

KARIM. African Violets, Vetiver, Bergamot Oil, Nile Spice ... Which one would you like to try? *(She moves closer to him.)*

MARINA. This one.

KARIM. And here's Ambergris, Civet, Sidi bu Said Jasmine ...

MARINA. This one.

KARIM. Here's Musk.

MARINA. Good.

MARINA. And this one?

KARIM. Marrakech Moon.

MARINA. And this?

KARIM. Tunisian Nights. *(Paquita enters with a few rugs and a carpet beater.)*

PAQUITA. Can you believe that I'm married to a perfumer and I can't wear any of his perfumes, because they all make me sneeze?

19

KARIM. And can you believe I'm married to a woman who doesn't even let me kiss her toes at night?

MARINA. Now I'm confused. You two are married?

PAQUITA. Never thought I could fish them that young, enh? *(Emiliano enters.)*

EMILIANO. Do you have the key to the cellar, Paquita?

MARINA. Are they really married, Papá?

EMILIANO. Yes, they are.

PAQUITA. Tell her how he beats me at night.

KARIM. And tell her how she's having an affair with the milkman.

MARINA. Stop! Tell me the truth.

PAQUITA. She doesn't believe us, Emiliano.

MARINA. No. I don't. You don't sleep in the same room. Papá, tell me the truth.

EMILIANO. Well, they are married but they are not married.

MARINA. What do you mean?

PAQUITA. I am stuck with this fool, until he gets his residency papers, then I can divorce him and marry your father.

EMILIANO. At the rate it's going we'll be seventy.

PAQUITA. Then I'll use my white hair as a veil. Here's the key. *(Emiliano exits.)*

MARINA. So what are you going to do when you become a Spanish citizen?

KARIM. Be another gypsy in this country.

PAQUITA. I told him he should go to school and study.

KARIM. *(Hands her another bottle.)* And what should I study? — Try this one.

PAQUITA. Something interesting like astronomy, architecture … You can study algebra. The Moors were good at algebra.

KARIM. A lot of good that would do me: X equals Morocco and Y equals Spain, and that equals the scalping of the Moors from this country in 1492. Solution to the problem, a thousand years have to pass, before a Moroccan can be on the same level as a Spaniard.

PAQUITA. That's not algebra.

KARIM. I can look around me and do the math.

MARINA. What's in this bottle, Karim? *(Emiliano enters again. He notices Karim and Marina.)*

PAQUITA. Those oriental oils are dangerous. You got to be careful when you go to the market with me.

MARINA. Why?

PAQUITA. We'll have many men following us everywhere.

MARINA. Good!

PAQUITA. No! Not when I'm shopping for food. Men and food don't go well together. They break my concentration, and I like to read the ingredients on the cans in peace.

MARINA. So what should I wear gardenia?

PAQUITA. Worse. Then we'll have bees following us.

EMILIANO. Let's go Karim.

MARINA. And this one?

KARIM. Janat Al Naim.

MARINA. I like how you say it. I'm buying this one. *(He starts to pick up the bottles. He makes a bundle with the arabesque cloth.)*

KARIM. Take it. It's a present from me. *(She offers him a smile.)*

EMILIANO. Let's go, if you want a ride from me. I'll be in the car. *(Emiliano exits.)*

MARINA. Janat al Naim. Some people should speak in different languages all day long, even if nobody understands them. They can begin a sentence in French and finish it in Mandarin. What counts is the sound of the words. The way the words sound like music. Karim, you are one of those people.

KARIM. Me?

MARINA. You have a way with language. Say something in Arabic or in French. *(Paquita begins to clean the rugs, as she listens to their conversation.)*

KARIM. What do you want me to say, something polite?

MARINA. Yes, something polite.

KARIM. *El-hamdulellah ennek gaity.*

MARINA. See how good it sounds: *El-hamdulellah ennek gaity.* What does it mean?

KARIM. Thank God you've come.

MARINA. And something impolite? Say something impolite.

KARIM. I got to go.

PAQUITA. Go or you'll make Emiliano late to his meeting.

KARIM. Your father is going to give me a ride. *Adios.*

MARINA. *El-hamdulellah ennek gaity.* How long have you known my father?

PAQUITA. Ah, many years. I met him standing in front of one of his paintings. I was looking at a picture and fell in love with him through his work. Your father and I ... We are like a couple, but we don't. *(Makes a discreet sexual gesture.)* None of that between us. Well, some nights, yes ... *(Remembers. Laughs.)* When we've been drinking, yes. But I love your father the same way I love a part of

21

myself. I love him the same way I admire something inside a glass case in a store. It's there behind the glass, and I don't have to buy it. It's better to look at it.

MARINA. Why?

PAQUITA. Ay! Maybe you won't understand. No. Maybe not, because you're young, and when you're young you live close to the skin, the flesh. I've moved to another part of my body. *(Chuckles.)* For me sex is like a summerhouse I closed up for the winter. That doesn't mean I won't go back. Yes sir, if a man sweeps me off my feet that's a different story. But now I prefer a companion. Your father understands me. You see that light over there. *(Points in the direction of the sea.)* You see. I love him like that. Like that light that is full of respect for life. *(Flamenco music plays.)*

Scene 4

Emiliano and Lorca enter talking.

EMILIANO. *(Shakes his head.)* I have to sleep. I have to go to bed. *(Looks at his watch.)* Look at the time! It's past five o'clock in the morning. And where's Marina and Karim? They've stayed out all night.

LORCA. They must still be out dancing.

EMILIANO. This late!

LORCA. Don't tell me you're going to start getting worried again! *(Emiliano paces the room.)*

EMILIANO. Of course I am! It's past five o'clock! The road from Granada is dangerous at night. There are too many curves and Karim likes to drink a little too much.

LORCA. Here, have some wine. *(Gives him a bottle of wine.)* It will calm you down. *(Lorca brings a chair and sits him down.)* Sit down. I'll cut your hair. *(Lorca takes his off his jacket and wraps it around him.)*

EMILIANO. I just had it cut. *(Pulls the jacket away.)*

LORCA. Then I'll give you a shave. *(Wraps the jacket around him again.)*

EMILIANO. Absolutely not!

LORCA. Then I'll trim the little hairs inside your nose.

EMILIANO. Don't you dare!

LORCA. Then take your brushes and paint!

EMILIANO. I can't paint when I'm anxious. *(Emiliano gets up from the chair.)*

LORCA. Come on, it will help you relax. *(Brings him a sketchpad.)* Sketch something. Let me find you a pencil. *(Runs to the table and rummages through his paints.)* I always confided to paper all my feelings. I'd free myself of my worries by writing poems or scenes for my sad puppets. *(Finds the pencil.)* Here's a pencil. I'll pose for you. I'll keep you company. Let me take off your shoes. *(Bends down to take off his shoes.)*

EMILIANO. No. Leave my shoes on!

LORCA. I'll massage your feet!

EMILIANO. No. Leave my feet alone! *(Paquita enters in a dressing gown. Emiliano moves away from Lorca and pretends to be dusting off his shoes.)*

PAQUITA. They haven't come home yet?

EMILIANO. No.

PAQUITA. Go to bed, Emiliano.

EMILIANO. I will. I will.

PAQUITA. Do you need anything?

EMILIANO. No. I'm fine. I'm fine.

PAQUITA. Do you want me to stay up with you?

EMILIANO. No, you rest. You rest …

PAQUITA. All right, *mi amor. (Emiliano paces the room.)*

LORCA. You know I was in love with a woman once, Ana Maria, Salvador Dalí's sister.

EMILIANO. And?

LORCA. I was in love with her brother first. *(Laughs.)* Ah, it was terrible. He was the one who introduced me to her. It was a little messy … Very messy.

EMILIANO. *(Looks at his watch.)* I just hope nothing happened! *(Lorca looks for something in his pocket.)*

LORCA. Here, I found this for you. *(Opens a paper and reads.)* "It is an offense to steal a nest or an egg. Contravention of this sort results in a fine."

EMILIANO. I've read it before …

LORCA. Then you know it's against the law …

EMILIANO. Are you a policeman now?

LORCA. No. God forbid! But it shows that you didn't grow up around here. It's bad luck to remove them.

EMILIANO. So am I cursed then? Is that why you're here, to take me away?

LORCA. Listen to that! Am I here to take him away? *(Laughs.)*

EMILIANO. Sometimes you scare the shit out of me. I've seen you as the angel of death in my dreams.

LORCA. The angel of death. *(Laughs.)* That's because you are painting my death, my friend. When an angel is assigned to a man who is about to die, much has happened already. Death could've been prepared a long time ago by a disease or a killer. The angel only arrives at the end. At the precise moment to kiss the dying man and inhale his breath. And you see, I'm here and you're not dying, unless you think you are.

EMILIANO. No, I'm not dying.

LORCA. Then are you going to take part in a duel that I should plan to attend?

EMILIANO. I don't think so.

LORCA. Well then, don't be paranoid? — Here, smoke. *(Lights him a cigarette.)* Blow out some of your worries and inquietude. *(Emiliano takes the cigarette and smokes.)* That's the problem with visiting the living. You always think we have ulterior motives. *(The sound of car doors being closed.)*

EMILIANO. Good, I think they're home. *(Emiliano goes out to meet Marina and Karim.)*

MARINA. *(Offstage.)* We drove all the way to Málaga. I didn't think it was such a big city. We met a couple from Madrid at a disco. *(Entering.)* They took us to a party. Then we went to another party. I've never danced so much in my life. I can't imagine living without dancing. Let's go to the beach, Karim. Let's go see the sunrise. Later, there'll be an eclipse.

EMILIANO. Aren't you tired? Don't you want to get some sleep?

MARINA. *(Prancing and swirling round the room.)* Who cares about sleep! Who wants to sleep! Tomorrow I'll sleep and the day after. I started to live again, Papá. Come with us to see the sunrise. You slept enough.

EMILIANO. I haven't slept a wink. I was worried.

MARINA. Papá, we're not children. Let's celebrate life. *(She takes her father by the hand and begins to dance with him.)*

EMILIANO. Marina, you've gone mad.

MARINA. Why? Don't you want to see me happy? *(She is twirling around with him.)* Dance with me. Who wants to sleep! We could die while sleeping. *(Paquita enters half-asleep.)*

24

PAQUITA. What's going on?

MARINA. *(Pulls her by the arm.)* Good. You're up. Let's go to the beach. Get ready.

PAQUITA. Where are we going?

EMILIANO. They just got in.

PAQUITA. And where are they taking me?

MARINA. To dance.

PAQUITA. I can't go like this. Can someone tell me what's happening?

MARINA. We're going to dance on the beach!

PAQUITA. Now? Ah no! I'm going back to bed! *(Paquita exits.)*

EMILIANO. *(Touches Marina's face.)* I'll make you something warm to drink.

MARINA. No. I'm going to change. I'll bring your music to the beach, Karim. *(Marina exits.)*

EMILIANO. What's going on?

KARIM. She wants to stay up.

EMILIANO. Is she high?

KARIM. She drank. We had a couple of drinks.

EMILIANO. Don't lie to me. What did she take?

KARIM. Let her be. The girl is enjoying herself. She was sad about her mother's death …

EMILIANO. And you're just as high as she is.

KARIM. Oh, come on!

EMILIANO. You can't even look at me straight in the eyes. What did you take? *(Pause.)* What did you take?

KARIM. Ecstasy.

EMILIANO. Karim!

KARIM. I didn't buy it.

EMILIANO. Of course you did. How would she know where to find it?

KARIM. No. She bought it and slipped it into my mouth.

EMILIANO. And you were stupid enough to swallow it. I'll have to talk to her.

KARIM. Don't make a big fuss! Let her be. And don't tell her I told you!

EMILIANO. I'll make her something warm to drink. *(He starts to exit.)*

KARIM. Emiliano.

EMILIANO. What?

KARIM. Would you come with me to Granada tomorrow? There's

25

something I want to show you. There's a store that's for rent on Tetería road.

EMILIANO. And?

KARIM. Let's open up a business.

EMILIANO. So this ecstasy drug gives you wild ideas.

KARIM. Oh, it's a beautiful store. Small. But it's got everything, glass cases and chairs. It used to be a jewelry shop. It even has a cash register. It would be a good place for a perfumery store. All the teashops are there. And all these other stores next to it that sell rugs and things from Morocco, my business will fit right in.

EMILIANO. I don't need any more work in my life.

KARIM. But it will be my work. I'll run the place. I'll manage it. Look, I'll pay you back …

EMILIANO. If I give you money, it's for you to go back to your country.

KARIM. Is that what you really want?

EMILIANO. Sometimes, yes.

KARIM. Why do you always say that? Why are you always threatening me, if you say you care for me? Come here. Give me a hug.

EMILIANO. You must really be high.

KARIM. It's not because I'm high. *(Reaches out to Emiliano and tries to hug him.)* Come here.

EMILIANO. *(Pulling away.)* Yes, you're high like a kite.

KARIM. *(Grabbing his hands.)* Give me a hug.

EMILIANO. So ecstasy makes her happy and makes you affectionate.

KARIM. No. It's not the drug. Come here.

EMILIANO. So what do you want from me? Why do you want a hug?

KARIM. Because I love you and you're like a father to me.

EMILIANO. *(With a sudden outburst.)* Come on, I'm not your father! I wish I could see you as a son. But that's not possible. Look, I told you I'd give you time to think, when you said you were confused about us, so it's up to you. Do you really want me to hug you? *(Opens his arms with desire.)*

LORCA. Ah, silence. I don't think he really wants the hug. At least not the one you would give him.

KARIM. It's all right. *(Karim moves to another part of the stage.)*

LORCA. Love is absurd, my friend. Who we love is not the person in front of us, but the person we have fixed in our mind and heart. We close our eyes, even when we sense danger and we smell the flowers of bleeding knives. We create our own night, so we can surrender ourselves to these strangers; in a night that covers all things, so logic can dissolve.

EMILIANO. I'll go get something warm for Marina. *(Emiliano exits. Karim paces the room lost in thought. Marina enters. She's dressed playfully. She wears one of Madame Gallimard's hats and a long silk scarf. She has brought a boom box and is playing soft techno music. She has brought three other hats.)*

MARINA. I'm ready for the beach. You wear this hat, Karim. *(Places the hat on his head.)* And I brought this one for Papá and this one for Paquita. *(Places the hat on his head.)* Do I look high?

KARIM. You look like you went to Pluto and back.

MARINA. Let's go to the beach.

KARIM. I think I'd much rather stay here.

MARINA. What happened?

KARIM. Nothing. Your father.

MARINA. But what happened?

KARIM. Nothing. Nothing. I want to rest. I have to make a delivery for your father tomorrow.

MARINA. *(Holds his hands.)* Oh, Karim, Karim, don't get sad on me.

KARIM. I'm not sad.

MARINA. Are you coming down from your high? *(Swirls him around.)* Karim, Karim, don't faint on me. Karim, Karim, what does your name mean?

KARIM. *(Smiles.)* My name?

MARINA. *(Playfully.)* Yes. What does it mean? What does it mean?

KARIM. *(Giving in to her.)* My name is one of the names of Allah.

MARINA. And how many names does Allah have?

KARIM. Two hundred and one names.

MARINA. And do they all have meaning?

KARIM. *(Nods.)* Karim means the generous one.

MARINA. And are you generous?

KARIM. I can be.

MARINA. Then come with me to the sea and tell me all the names of Allah and their meaning.

KARIM. *(With sensuality.)* And what would you give me in return?

MARINA. I will tell you the names of all my cousins.

KARIM. That wouldn't be fair.

MARINA. Why not? I'm sure all of your cousins were named after Allah.

KARIM. But I think you only have two cousins.

MARINA. Then I will give you the last thing we do when we make the sign of the cross.

KARIM. And what is that?

MARINA. We kiss the point of our fingers.

KARIM. So you're going to give me kisses in return?

MARINA. Yes, for every name you tell me.

KARIM. I like this game. That's two hundred and one kisses.

MARINA. Begin.

KARIM. Muhammed, the most praised one. *(Marina kisses his buttocks.)* Don't give me a kiss there.

MARINA. I'm not religious.

KARIM. But it's offensive to me.

MARINA. Then here. *(Kisses his hand. He begins to seduce her with the names.)*

KARIM. Ahmad, the ever-existing. *(Marina kisses his forehead.)* Munir, the illuminator of the world. *(Marina kisses his eyes.)* Mad'u, the one who accepted the call of Allah. *(Marina kisses his knees.)* Shafi, the one who cures sick hearts.

MARINA. That should be your name. *(Kisses the place close to his heart. He looks at her intensely.)*

KARIM. Kashif al-Karb, the one who erases pain and affliction. *(Marina blows him a kiss and traces the silhouette of his body. Karim brings her close to him.)* Fatih, the one who opens the door of hearts. *(He kisses her on the lips.)* Kamil, the perfect one. *(She returns his kiss.)*

MARINA. Let's go to the sea. *(They exit. Lorca takes a few steps forward. He shakes his head in disbelief. Emiliano enters the space with a glass of warm milk.)*

EMILIANO. Where are they?

LORCA. They've gone to the sea.

EMILIANO. I'll go find them. *(Emiliano starts to exit. Lorca stops him.)*

LORCA. No, don't go. Don't go all the way out there.

EMILIANO. But I've made her something warm to drink.

LORCA. She doesn't want anything. Give it to me. I'll take it. *(Lorca takes the glass of milk.)*

EMILIANO. What are you doing?

LORCA. We'll give it to the cat. Here kitty, kitty, kitty …

EMILIANO. I don't have a cat.

LORCA. Then we'll give it to the ants.

EMILIANO. But I just warmed it up for my daughter.

LORCA. Ants like it better when it's warm. Here, little ones.

EMILIANO. Agh! I'll go look for them. *(Emiliano begins to exit.)*
LORCA. Emiliano, stay here! Come back! Emiliano! ... *Joder.*
(Emiliano exits. Music plays.)

Scene 5

Paquita enters the stage wearing sunglasses and a hat.

PAQUITA. Marina, bring your sunglasses so you can watch. Soon everything will turn dark with the eclipse. *(Marina enters.)*
MARINA. It's incredible, this universe.
PAQUITA. Yes, full of mysteries. — You didn't sleep.
MARINA. Who needs sleep? We should be grateful and glad that we are alive.
PAQUITA. I am. I wake up every morning full of gratitude.
MARINA. Me too. Every day, every hour, every minute I feel I want to help the world. You did something good for Karim by marrying him.
PAQUITA. Oh, I'm like that sometimes, crazy as a goat!
MARINA. I imagine it must be hard getting a job if you're not a citizen of this country. I know it's very difficult in the States.
PAQUITA. Oh, but I did it for your father. Your father asked me if I could marry the Moroccan and help him out. And I know life isn't easy in his country. Then I looked at the boy's face — that smile he has like a piece of bread, and I looked at your father. And of course, I have a heart the size of a watermelon. The next thing I was wearing a corsage and standing in front of a notary marrying the boy. But I did it to keep up appearances, in this small town, where the air is thick and unkind, because people pollute it with gossip and evil thoughts. I did it for your father, so he can be with Karim.
MARINA. *(In a state of shock.)* What? I didn't know Karim was with my father ...
PAQUITA. Ah, but you certainly know ... I mean, you do know that some men like your father like to ... I don't know how to say it ... Fraternize.
MARINA. Of course I know ... .
PAQUITA. Ah, good! For a minute I thought ...

MARINA. But I didn't know that my father and Karim ... Doesn't he work here?

PAQUITA. Yes, he helps your father with his work, but ...

MARINA. *(Looks into the distance.)* How could he not tell me? I guess I really don't know my father. He's always been a stranger to me. *(Emiliano and Lorca enter.)*

EMILIANO. Ah, you're here.

PAQUITA. Yes. We're here to see the eclipse. Do you have your sunglasses?

EMILIANO. No. I forgot them.

PAQUITA. Well, you need your sunglasses. Go in and get them. *(Emiliano looks disheveled, as if he hasn't slept.)*

EMILIANO. No, it's fine. I don't ... I'm not staying. I've seen many in my lifetime.

MARINA. Stay.

PAQUITA. Stay. I'll get your glasses. I'll get them for you. *(Paquita exits. There's an awkward silence between the father and daughter.)*

EMILIANO. Have you been up all this time?

MARINA. Yes.

EMILIANO. Marina, you can't be doing drugs.

MARINA. I know. But it was just one time. I promise ... *(Karim enters. He's been swimming. He wears shorts and a towel around his neck.)*

KARIM. The water is warm. You should swim. I'm going in to get a drink. You want something?

MARINA. No.

KARIM. And you? *(Karim exits.)*

MARINA. *(After a pause.)* Tell me about you and Karim? Paquita told me ...

EMILIANO. I don't want to talk about it.

MARINA. I'm sorry. I didn't know that you and him ...

EMILIANO. Well, now you know.

MARINA. If I had known, Papá ...

EMILIANO. It's better if we don't talk about it. *(Silence. He looks into the distance full of pain and remorse.)*

MARINA. Mamá and I always talked. Even towards the end, we talked about everything.

EMILIANO. So did she tell you about me?

MARINA. Yes, and sometimes she was very angry.

EMILIANO. Did it change the way you feel about me? You don't exactly have your so-called ordinary father.

MARINA. And what kind is that?

EMILIANO. Perhaps a man that looks and acts like Gregory Peck in *To Kill a Mockingbird*.

MARINA. Then I wouldn't be the proper daughter for him. *(A slight pause. Emiliano looks at her.)*

EMILIANO. Why Karim?

MARINA. Perhaps I have inherited my father's eyes.

EMILIANO. Not my best feature.

MARINA. The same could be said of my heart. *(This is quite embarrassing for her. There are tears in her eyes.)*

EMILIANO. An honest man would never do what he's doing, in front of my eyes, with my own daughter.

MARINA. Don't you think the same could be said of me?

EMILIANO. But you said you didn't know.

MARINA. No. He never told me and neither did you.

EMILIANO. Maybe you shouldn't have come! *(Karim enters.)*

KARIM. Is it happening yet? *(They all look up.)*

MARINA. Yes. The sky is starting to change.

KARIM. I've never seen an eclipse before.

MARINA. Neither have I. *(Paquita enters.)*

PAQUITA. Here are your glasses. Look, it's starting to happen. Put on your glasses. *(They all put their sunglasses on and look at the sky, except Emiliano. Sound of birds flapping their wings. Emiliano looks at Karim and Marina.)* Hear the birds. They think that night is coming our way. All the animals in the world will think that it's nighttime. *(A delicate but strange sound is heard, like the sound that is heard when one rubs the rim of a wineglass. Lorca enters wearing sunglasses.)*

LORCA. Yes, it's starting to change. The universe is astir and everything that exists is in motion. Even the heart is built in such a way that movement is its climate, and we can all be affected by this brief obscurity, because we each have our own little orbit. Ah, the eclipse! Evidence that the sky can be arrested, when the moon passes between the sun and the earth! *(The sound swells as orange lights begin to change into an array of blue and white lights. Then darkness begins to descend like a cloak of shadows covering the earth.)*

End of Act One

31

ACT TWO

Scene 1

Flamenco music. There is a large pile of broken objects. This pile sits on a platform with wheels. The family is having a picnic next to the pile, celebrating San Juan's Day. There's a tablecloth spread on the floor. There's wine, bread with sausage and fruits. All the characters have been drinking, but they are not drunk. They are laughing loudly. Emiliano is dancing to the music. He holds a bottle. Paquita joins him in the dance. She takes a cloth napkin and wraps it around his neck as she circles him. Karim and Marina are clapping. Lorca enters. He holds the moon on a leash. The moon floats like a balloon.

LORCA. Five o'clock in the afternoon. Ah, laughter in the air! That's it, Emiliano, laugh and dance. It is necessary to laugh and invite the stars to swim in your belly, because it's all right if a man laughs from gladness, and lets a flock of birds fly out of his mouth. Laugh, laugh … That's it, Emiliano! Today I have the moon on a leash, and later when it's dark we will take her for a walk. *(The song finishes. The family applauds. Lorca waves at Emiliano. Paquita notices Lorca. She waves back.)*
PAQUITA. Who is that interesting man dressed in white?
EMILIANO. *(Pretending not to see him.)* I don't see anybody.
PAQUITA. He looks like he's from another time.
EMILIANO. He's probably an eclipse gazer. There are lots of crazies out this week.
PAQUITA. But he waved at me. It's strange, a man his age with a white balloon.
EMILIANO. Don't stare, Paquita! Don't stare, Marina! He's probably holding the balloon for his little girl who's collecting shells by the seashore.
MARINA. He must be a foreigner.

EMILIANO. He must know that we're talking about him. Don't stare. *(Lorca waves at them.)*

PAQUITA. *(Waves back.)* He waved at me again. I should ask him if he wants bread and sausage.

EMILIANO. No!

MARINA. Why not, Papá?

EMILIANO. Because he might be a vegetarian, and I'm not in the mood to socialize ...

PAQUITA. Ay, how strange you are, Emiliano!

KARIM. Never mind, he's gone.

EMILIANO. Now where were we, before you made me dance like a fool?

PAQUITA. Marina, what spices did you use on the food today? Emiliano hasn't stopped talking since we started eating.

EMILIANO. What's the matter, you don't like me to talk? Pass me another piece of sausage.

PAQUITA. I know that parsley makes parrots talk. Did you use lots of parsley?

MARINA. You were talking about your feet!

PAQUITA. Ay, don't talk about your feet when we are eating and drinking!

KARIM. Why not?

PAQUITA. Because it is not proper!

KARIM. We're not going to eat his feet. Unless you feel an unbearable desire to eat them. *(Laughter.)*

PAQUITA. You have no manners, Karim. *(Takes his wineglass.)* No more wine for you.

KARIM. Give me back my wine.

PAQUITA. This one drinks a glass of wine then he doesn't know what he's saying. *(Paquita drinks from his glass.)*

KARIM. Did you see that? She drank my wine and she says I have no manners. You might want to hide your feet. She might eat them.

PAQUITA. Well, I do like to eat pig feet. *(They laugh.)*

EMILIANO. Ha! The truth comes out. We find out who has a foot fetish. *(Emiliano taps his glass with a spoon, as if to make a toast.)* Señoras y señores, we have a feet eater at our table!

PAQUITA. You bastard!

EMILIANO. Tonight, hide your feet under the covers. *(She takes her napkin and starts to hit him. Emiliano runs off and she runs after him. Karim and Marina are alone now.)*

KARIM. *(Grabs her arm.)* Why are you avoiding me?

MARINA. Because I don't want to talk to you or see you again!

KARIM. Why? *(We hear laughter. Marina moves away from him. Emiliano and Paquita enter the stage laughing.)*

PAQUITA. All right, I'm ready to start the fire.

EMILIANO. But the sun is still out.

PAQUITA. This is when we light fires on San Juan's day. That's how it was done in my town. This is my favorite holiday, because it's a way of cleansing life and making room for new things to come. On San Juan's Day we make a fire, Marina, and burn things that are no longer of any use to us. We feed the flames torn dresses, old gloves, combs with missing teeth, broken chairs. We burn old dreams, broken nights, broken love, and the fire burns like a hungry volcano eating away everything we feed it. For many years I have burned men on San Juan's Day.

EMILIANO. *(Playfully.)* Oh, there she goes! *(They all laugh. Paquita takes a swig from the bottle.)*

PAQUITA. It's true!

EMILIANO. How many men? How many?

PAQUITA. Many! Men who did me wrong: Tito Carnero, Chucho Escalante, Juan Jose Amado, Melino Tucci ... Can't forget him! The Sardinian carpenter who was full of dreams and wanted to build me a bungalow by the sea. Rodrigo Bagaria, that was another one ... Pascual Trinidad. My fires like eating men the most. *(Laughs.)* Or rather it's me who takes pleasure in seeing them burn in the flames.

MARINA. And how do you burn the men?

PAQUITA. No. I don't actually burn them. I burn something that represents them, a little token or something. It could be a shoelace, an old love letter ... Come on, today I feel like burning everything. Let's find more stuff and build the bonfire. *(To Emiliano.)* Emiliano, get your rifle.

EMILIANO. What?

PAQUITA. We have to shoot into the air to celebrate. *(Paquita, Marina and Karim exit. Emiliano approaches Lorca.)*

EMILIANO. I'll be there in a second.

LORCA. *Hola,* Emiliano!

EMILIANO. You were waving at us.

LORCA. I was being cordial.

EMILIANO. I noticed. Everybody saw you and then you disappeared like a ghost.

LORCA. And how else do you want me to disappear?

34

EMILIANO. This is not the time — (*Paquita and Marina enter with objects and wood in their arms.*)

PAQUITA. Emiliano, get moving!

EMILIANO. I'm going.

PAQUITA. (*To Marina.*) Get more wood. (*Karim enters with an armful of wood.*)

KARIM. (*To Marina as he smiles.*) You want me to help you?

PAQUITA. She doesn't need any help. (*Emiliano, Lorca and Marina exit. Paquita takes a white shirt from a paper bag.*) I'm burning this shirt.

KARIM. That's mine.

PAQUITA. Yes, I know and I'm burning it.

KARIM. Give me that! (*He tries to grab the shirt, but she pulls her arm away.*)

PAQUITA. Don't think I haven't noticed what's going on between you and Marina! And don't think I don't know what happened between you and Emiliano! At the beginning you pretended to be all love. Then you dropped him by saying that your religion didn't allow it. Of course, after I was stupid enough to marry you.

KARIM. Why don't you mind your own business! (*Karim starts to exit.*)

PAQUITA. I'll mind my own business when we're divorced and everything has been straightened out by the law. You hear me! (*Paquita holds the shirt up in the air. In a loud voice:*) Ay, San Juan, may your fire vanish him from here!

Ay, San Juan, may the divorce papers come through soon!

Ay, San Juan, make him disappear once and for all! (*Emiliano enters with Marina. He holds a rifle.*)

EMILIANO. Who are you getting rid of?

PAQUITA. (*In a loud voice as she exits.*) Do I have to tell you? Do I have to? Let me find more things to burn. Today I feel the devil in me!

EMILIANO. Well, don't burn down the house! (*Laughs.*) She's liable to burn down the whole place, if you let her.

MARINA. And what are you burning?

EMILIANO. (*Dismissively.*) Agh! It's all a myth, an old tradition. What am I doing with this gun? I don't believe in these things.

MARINA. I'd like to believe in something.

EMILIANO. And what would you like to burn?

MARINA. If these bonfires release anything into the air, there's a lot we should burn. And we should start from the beginning.

EMILIANO. And what's the beginning for you?

MARINA. It would have to be the day you left home — What do you remember most about the child you left behind? *(He is not willing to recall any dark memories. He smiles and looks at her full of love and tenderness.)*

EMILIANO. You didn't like going to sleep at night. I always had to carry you in my arms and take you for long walks.

MARINA. And the mother? *(He looks into the distance as they both enter more delicate territory. They speak to each other like two old friends.)*

EMILIANO. The mother ... the mother was unkind to me. She was awful to me at the end.

MARINA. Was it because you had stopped seeing her as a woman?

EMILIANO. You should've asked your mother when she was alive.

MARINA. So why didn't you write for so many years?

EMILIANO. Your mother kept moving to different countries with her job —

MARINA. You could've contacted the United Nations where she worked —

EMILIANO. Don't you think your mother should've done that?

MARINA. She did a lot. Bless her heart.

EMILIANO. Yes, that was part of the problem. She did too much!

MARINA. She had to! You left! You weren't around!

EMILIANO. *(With sudden explosion.)* And how was I supposed to be around! How was I supposed to be around, when she was always making it impossible for me to see you!

MARINA. You were busy yourself, Papa. You were trying to make it as a painter.

EMILIANO. Yes, I was trying to make it as a painter! So what does that have to do with it?

MARINA. You probably didn't need the extra burden of a child on your shoulders.

EMILIANO. That's not true, Marina.

MARINA. Then why didn't you take her to court?

EMILIANO. For what, so she could accuse me of being a faggot? *(More contained now.)* Look, you were too young to remember.

MARINA. No. I was eight going on twenty! Don't tell me I wasn't old enough!

EMILIANO. I'm sorry. I didn't mean ...

MARINA. *(There are tears in her eyes.)* No. I shouldn't have brought it up. It's just that sometimes her death is like a hood over my face.

I think of her all the time. I see her everywhere and everything I do. She appears all of a sudden in my thoughts. The sight of her face. The color of her lipstick. *(Emiliano tries to ease the situation and smiles faintly.)*

EMILIANO. Well, she always knew how to choose the right color of lipstick.

MARINA. *(Laughs tenderly.)* Yes, it was called Red Roulette, like the red in casinos. The kind of red that would make you bet your life on her lips. *(Becomes more serious.)* Sometimes I think I'm obsessed with her, and I want to understand why she did all this. Why she kept me from you?

EMILIANO. I always thought it was punishment. You were her ammunition, her way of getting back at me.

MARINA. But couldn't she see that she was also punishing me?

EMILIANO. No.

MARINA. Maybe she still saw a part of you in me.

EMILIANO. I hope so. You're also my daughter.

MARINA. Then she still loved you through me.

EMILIANO. Can you call that love?

PAQUITA. *(We hear Paquita calling Marina from a distance.)* Marina! Come help me! Marina!

MARINA. I should go. *(Marina kisses her father and exits. Emiliano stays looking at her full of love and affection. Lorca enters.)*

LORCA. *Hola, hombre ...*

EMILIANO. Ah you ...

LORCA. Yes, me. I'm still here.

EMILIANO. Always observing.

LORCA. Yes, that is much of what I do now. Let's go for a walk. *(Reaches out to him.)*

EMILIANO. No. Not tonight. Not now. Do you think I've been selfish with my work and my life?

LORCA. Why do you say that? An artist needs to be selfish. An artist needs his individual freedom as much as he needs air to breathe.

EMILIANO. Is that why I have failed as a father?

LORCA. I wouldn't say that, my friend. I believe that as a father you yielded to circumstances. Am I wrong in saying this? Or were you willing to tear your daughter away from a home where she was happy and content?

EMILIANO. No.

LORCA. And I imagine you didn't want to battle with the mother in court and have the child go through all that nonsense.

EMILIANO. You're right.

LORCA. Then there's your answer. You preferred to sacrifice yourself. Don't you think that's the opposite of being selfish?

EMILIANO. *(Shakes his head. Walks.)* Sometimes I feel like I live three lives, as three different people, with three souls, three hearts and three minds: There is the artist in me who lives a private life, a solitary life of colors and inner thoughts; then there is my darker side, a lonely life, a life that looks for other men who share my same desires; then there is my life as a father, which I really don't know, which was taken away from me. I mean, how does one learn to be a father?

LORCA. My friend, it doesn't do you much good to accuse yourself of being a failure. *(Pats him on the shoulder.)* You are an artist and that's like being a father to many children. Consider the heart doctor, who has listened to more than a million heartbeats, but never really gets to understand the secret language of hearts. Consider the barber who cuts hair, but his comb never reaches beyond the mass of curls to man's deepest thoughts. But you are a creator and artists sometimes tap into the mystery of all these things. — The problem too, is that we're condemned to solitude. — Come on let's light the fire. Let's burn the past. Let us observe the dancing flames. Ah, there's so much I'd like to burn. Let's light the fire, *hombre!* Rituals are important. We need beginnings and endings. *(Lorca lights the fire. A surreal orange and yellow light begins to emerge from the pile of objects. Flamenco music also begins to rise from the flames.)* Let's see the laughter of the flames. The fervor. The eloquence of light! Dance with me!

EMILIANO. You're mad!

LORCA. No. Dance with me! Let it burn! *(Lorca begins to dance whimsically. He grabs Emiliano by the arm and both men begin to dance around the fire. Paquita enters with a bottle of wine.)*

PAQUITA. You lit the fire without me.

LORCA. *(Pulls her to dance.)* Come and dance with us. *(They speak to each other loudly over the music as they dance. The music swells. The three of them dance in a circle.)*

PAQUITA. Who are you? Who is your friend, Emiliano?

LORCA. I am an actor!

PAQUITA. He knows how to dance!

EMILIANO. Yes, he is an actor playing Lorca in a play.

PAQUITA. He does looks like him!

LORCA. Ah, yes I do! That's what everybody says!

PAQUITA. Where are you performing?

LORCA. I am performing in a theatre called the world!

PAQUITA. Ah, he's kidding!

EMILIANO. No, he's not. He plays everywhere. He tours.

PAQUITA. Ah! Let's go see him perform.

EMILIANO. We can't. Tonight was his last performance.

PAQUITA. Ah! What a shame!

LORCA. It doesn't matter. There'll be others.

PAQUITA. Then let us drink and dance the whole night! *(She hands the wine bottle to Lorca, but Emiliano takes it from him.)*

EMILIANO. He can't. He must travel to another town tomorrow. *(Emiliano takes a swig from the bottle.)*

LORCA. That's right. Barcelona, Madrid, Salamanca ... The moon ...

PAQUITA. Ah! The moon ...

LORCA. *Que viva el dia de San Juan!*

PAQUITA. *Que viva San Juan! (The three of them exit dancing. Marina and Karim enter. She holds the bottle of perfume he gave her.)*

MARINA. Janat al Naim. Is Janat al Naim another name for God?

KARIM. No. Why do you ask?

MARINA. Because I just poured all the perfume into the fire.

KARIM. Do you know that when...?

MARINA. Yes. I know — What is my father to you?

KARIM. Your father? He is like a father to me.

MARINA. Paquita told me something different.

KARIM. *(Becomes defensive.)* Paquita says many things! What does she know about me, enh? I never had a father or a mother, enh? My aunt brought me up. My real mother and father died when I was young. I really don't have any family. That's why your father is like a father to me.

MARINA. Then I'd have to get used to you being my brother.

KARIM. That would be very difficult. *(He moves close to her full of love.)*

MARINA. No. I'm looking at you now and we could pass —

KARIM. Impossible. *(She tries to see him as a brother now, even though this is painful for her. She messes his hair as a way of expressing her change of heart. He knows what she is doing and he won't fall for it. He grabs her arm.)* Come here, *habibi* —

MARINA. No. Stand there. We have to leave this place and walk backwards. We have to go back to that first day, when I arrived in

Granada and start all over again …

KARIM. Why are you saying all this?

MARINA. *(Sudden burst.)* Because I'm trying to figure out how to do it! Because I'm trying to pretend to be your sister! Because that's the way things are and I'm angry at myself for being weak and stupid!

KARIM. *(He grabs her arm.)* Come here, *habibi,* I have a friend who has a room. We could meet there. It overlooks the Alhambra. It is very beautiful. You would like it there.

MARINA. No. My father will be there in that room. Everywhere I'd look I would see him. In every window. In every wall. Why didn't you tell me about him?

KARIM. Because there was nothing to tell you, and everything happened so fast, like falling. When you're falling you don't even have time to think because it happens so fast.

MARINA. But it's my father we're talking about.

KARIM. Look, we can meet away from here. My friend Hamid, he meets his girl there. He calls it his *garçonnier.*

MARINA. Does he also live with a man?

KARIM. Why are you asking me this?

MARINA. I'm trying to understand!

KARIM. Look, it was my first time and I didn't like it!

MARINA. And why didn't you walk away from the whole thing?

KARIM. Because, because one thing led to another as with you. It was light outside, and all of a sudden it turned dark. And your father said I could stay over. And I did. I stayed in the room where you sleep now. *(It's embarrassing for him to provide her with more details. He turns the conversation in another direction, because she is the only thing that matters now, and he tries desperately to win her back.)* I remember the whole room was waiting for you. All the furniture. Everything waited for you. The windows. The curtains. Everything waited for the day that you would occupy it.

MARINA. You're making it sound as if my father was setting us up, even before we met.

KARIM. No, I think I imagined you that night. There were pictures of you in the room. *(He is holding the tip of her chin. Emiliano enters.)*

EMILIANO. Marina. *(The young lovers separate.)*

MARINA. Yes.

EMILIANO. Why don't you join us! I opened another bottle of wine.

MARINA. We'll be there in a minute. *(Emiliano exits.)* Let's forget about everything. I came here to be with my father, not to steal you away from him.

KARIM. *(Grabs her by the elbow.)* Look, whatever was there, it's over. Trust me!

MARINA. But not for my father! *(She has left the room through her mind.)* What if I ask you to do something?

KARIM. Do what?

MARINA. To be with him as before.

KARIM. Oh, come on! What are you saying! Do you even care for me? You're asking me to do the impossible!

MARINA. *(Suddenly exploding.)* You've also asked me to do the impossible! You're asking me to be with you knowing that my father is there! *(Silence.)*

KARIM. Tell me, why you want me to go back with your father?

MARINA. Because I want to do for him what he couldn't do for me. Because I want to show him that I accept him for who he is.

KARIM. And if I do what you're asking me to do, where does this leave us?

MARINA. I'd teach you to love him as much as you love me. *(He moves closer to her.)*

KARIM. And how would you do that, if you know that I'm crazy about you?

MARINA. I will teach you little by little. *(He can't resist her. He touches her face tenderly. She is just as weak as he is. She looks at him tenderly and lets her fingers run over his shoulders.)* You only have to love him as if he were a woman. A man. A horse. The moon. You only have to tell him all the sacred names in your mouth, until all the names become one word, one sound, unbound from above, ancient and sacred as all the names of God. *(They are both transfixed.)*

KARIM. Marina. I want to tell you these things. I can only tell them to you.

MARINA. *(Touches his hair. There are tears in her eyes.)* And why can't it be as if I were giving you to him? As a present. A box full of you.

KARIM. And us? *(Marina pulls away from him and starts to exit. He runs after her.)* And us? Answer me. Marina. — Look, I'll do whatever you ask me to do. I'll go back with him, if that's what you want. I'll do it for you. I'll do it for you, if you'll have me back. Marina … Marina … *(Paquita and Emiliano enter.)*

PAQUITA. Where is that actor friend of yours? I liked him.

EMILIANO. Ah, he had to go.

PAQUITA. I'd like to dance with him again. *(All of a sudden Emiliano sees her beauty. He looks at her with desire.)*
EMILIANO. You look beautiful in this light.
PAQUITA. I do. You evil man! *(Playfully.)* Why do you always tell me beautiful things when you drink? *(He becomes playful and takes her by the hand to dance.)*
EMILIANO. Because I hear a foxtrot, then you're a woman and I'm a man and — *(Sings.)* Tah tah, ta tah … Ta ra ra ra rah …
PAQUITA. And how come I hear a tango?
EMILIANO. Ah, you hear a tango! *(Changes the dance steps and tune.)* Tan, tan, tan, tah, tanh …
PAQUITA. With you I'm sadly happy. Whatever that means. *(All of a sudden her eyes fill with tears.)* With you I'm as sad and happy as I've never been before.
EMILIANO. Then we need a rrrumba to take away the sadness.
PAQUITA. No, no rumba. Nothing. Nothing. Silent music. The music of our breath.
EMILIANO. And how do we dance to our breath?
PAQUITA. Like this. *(She places her head next to his chest. They kiss passionately. Then he pulls away from her.)*
EMILIANO. Good night, my dear. I love you. *(He turns away from her and begins to exit. Paquita stays looking at him in her desolation. Fado music plays. Lights shift.)*

Scene 2

Lorca holds a hand puppet of a man dressed in a black suit, which he manipulates. He begins to play the guessing game with the puppet.

LORCA. You and I will play the guessing game. And if it were a tree?
PUPPET. It would have to be an olive tree.
LORCA. If it were a building?
PUPPET. The Alhambra.
LORCA. And if it were an object?
PUPPET. An umbrella.
LORCA. Why an umbrella?

PUPPET. Because if I cry, you would have to use an umbrella.
LORCA. Why?
PUPPET. Because when I cry, it rains.
LORCA. Why?
PUPPET. Because I have eyes made out of clouds.
LORCA. Ah, so you're a sad puppet.
PUPPET. No. I'm a happy puppet.
LORCA. What would you like to see on the stage?
PUPPET. *Hamlet.*
LORCA. *Hamlet?* What about my plays?
PUPPET. I didn't see your plays.
LORCA. You never saw my plays?
PUPPET. I never saw your plays.
LORCA. Shshsh ... Someone's coming! *(Emiliano enters. To the puppet.)* This is Emiliano. And this is Hilario.
EMILIANO. Good to meet you.
PUPPET. Is he the painter you were talking about?
EMILIANO. Probably.
LORCA. Don't ask so many questions and go to sleep! Go to sleep!
EMILIANO. Here, there are two articles written on the newspapers this morning about the exhumation of the mass graves.
LORCA. I read them. Or do you think I don't read the papers?
EMILIANO. So your family is against all this.
LORCA. It's difficult for them.
EMILIANO. But can't they realize that Federico García Lorca doesn't just belong to the García Lorca family. Don't they realize that you belong to the world, history?
LORCA. Nothing will come of this. You can rest assured. Hundreds of years have to pass. Many years.
EMILIANO. Have you been here for a long time?
LORCA. Long enough to observe some of the things that are going on in this house with your family.
EMILIANO. And what have you observed?
LORCA. Nothing that you haven't noticed! Just be careful with that boy. He seems lost — Do you know that sometimes I feel that something solid has remained in me?
EMILIANO. And what is that?
LORCA. Sometimes I think there's a room left open, a space in my being for a love life.
EMILIANO. And who do you want to fall in love with?
LORCA. Not a human being.

EMILIANO. Then what?

LORCA. Maybe a guitar, or a painting, or a ship. Humans are too complicated. *(Lorca puts the puppet away. Emiliano begins to paint.)*

EMILIANO. What did happen between you and the painter Dalí?

LORCA. One day I tried to kiss the bastard and he had a coughing fit. *(Laughs.)* He said he was terrified of tongues because they reminded him of wiggling hearts.

EMILIANO. And the sculptor you were in love with?

LORCA. Have you ever seen an animal gnawing and tearing apart a piece of flesh?

EMILIANO. I get the picture.

LORCA. It's always been a bullfight and someone has to suffer the little stream of blood. *(Karim enters.)*

KARIM. Emiliano.

EMILIANO. Yes.

KARIM. I'd like to talk to you.

LORCA. Be kind, Emiliano. I think this boy is hurting. See him as if he were asleep.

   If we see all beings as if they were asleep, then we see them as children.

   And one can always find innocence in a child.

EMILIANO. I'd also like to have a conversation with you.

LORCA. Good. You'll find patience and the right words.

EMILIANO. So you start? What do you want to talk about?

KARIM. Well I … I don't know how … I don't know how to begin … I've been thinking, you see.

LORCA. Be careful, Emiliano.

KARIM. Do you remember when you bought all the cement and we started fixing the house? Those were good times we spent together.

EMILIANO. Yes, they were.

KARIM. We should fix what's broken between us. *(Silence.)*

LORCA. I think it's a little more complex with human beings.

KARIM. We could always try. *(Emiliano walks to another part of the terrace.)*

LORCA. Silence. Good.

EMILIANO. You know, it takes a long time to forget a person. A long time.

   And sometimes distance is better. It makes it go faster. Distance and time are alike, because they both heal. They both possess mysterious remedies.

And of course, I don't have any distance because you live here, so this has been the challenge.

KARIM. I know. You said this before and I'm sorry.

EMILIANO. Don't be sorry. How would we do this? How would we fix it?

KARIM. We could always go back to that first night. I remember you invited me here and you fed me. Then you asked me how much I charged. And I told you, nothing.

EMILIANO. It would've been better if you had charged me.

KARIM. Then I wouldn't have stayed.

EMILIANO. That's precisely my point.

KARIM. *(With sensuality.)* But I did stay and it turned dark outside; and you told me that I could sleep in Marina's room.

EMILIANO. I'd like to understand how this whole thing happened, this desire of yours for Marina, my own daughter.

KARIM. Emiliano, I didn't come here to talk …

EMILIANO. Oh, come on, Karim! Do you think I haven't noticed? I mean … you do realize that sooner or later you would have to face me. I am her father. I was actually looking at you and Marina this morning, standing next to each other, and I thought to myself, they actually look good together. They actually make a good couple. I don't know how it's done in Morocco. I know in some places the groom presents himself in front of the bride's house with a group of musicians. Pin … pi … rinh … pin … pinh … tin … tanh … Music and celebration. Don't tell me these were some of your plans, and I have ruined your surprise?

KARIM. *(Sudden burst.)* WHY DON'T YOU GIVE ME A BREAK HERE! I'M TRYING TO TELL YOU SOMETHING. I'M TRYING TO TALK TO YOU.

EMILIANO. And so am I.

LORCA. Another silence.

KARIM. Look, I didn't come here to talk about Marina.

EMILIANO. Then what? You expect me to believe you wanted to get back with me? I mean, how long were you going to keep Marina a secret?

KARIM. It's not what you think it is.

EMILIANO. You're lying! You have a habit of creating these phantoms and relationships in your mind. You bring people into your life, you assign them roles and then you change your mind and drop them. Is this what you are doing to Marina now? Tell me! Because I won't allow you to do this! You could do that to me. But

45

not her ... not her, you hear me?

KARIM. Emiliano, please!

EMILIANO. Tomorrow I want you gone from this house!

KARIM. You're throwing me out?

EMILIANO. Yes. And that's all there's to it! *(Karim is completely enraged. He shakes his head and paces back and forth.)*

KARIM. I feel sorry for you, Emiliano.

EMILIANO. I don't care how you feel about me.

KARIM. Always the same ... Exactly the same ... In your mind ... from the beginning ... Mistrust ... Something lurking inside your head, as if at any moment I was going to steal from you ...

EMILIANO. You have! You stole a lot from me. And each time you took more and more ...

KARIM. See, you've always seen me as a thief, haven't you? *(Lorca pats Emiliano on the shoulder, as if telling him to keep his calm.)* You live in fear like the rich. They are always frightened to lose what they have, and that's you Emiliano! You've always kept me at bay. Throwing me little pieces of crumbs, so I don't get ahead in the world. Never giving me too much — worried that if I have a little too much, I might get on with my life and leave you. That's you! You even tried to control my future, because you think I'm a nomad. A gypsy. You think that's part of who I am and where I come from. You think we all carry our houses on our backs like snails. Don't look at me that way. That's you, puffed up with prejudice and pride! You've always seen me as a crook, haven't you?

EMILIANO. Yes. And now I see you as being nothing. Nothing! And we have nothing else to talk about!

KARIM. What a sad person you are, solitary and sad with your sketches, your paintings and nests. *(Karim knocks down some of the nests and a painting. Marina and Paquita enter.)*

MARINA. Is everything all right, Papá?

KARIM. Your father just threw me out of the house.

EMILIANO. That's right!

KARIM. Are you coming with me?

EMILIANO. How dare you!

KARIM. I'm not talking to you. I'm talking to Marina. *(To Marina.)* I'll go pick up my things. You think about it. *(Karim starts to exit.)*

PAQUITA. What happened, Emiliano?

EMILIANO. I don't want him here and I want him far from you.*(Gestures to Marina.)*

PAQUITA. Yes, don't you dare go with him! *(Karim enters. He's holding a bundle that contains all of his merchandise.)*

KARIM. I heard that, Paquita.

PAQUITA. Good! I'm giving her my opinion.

KARIM. Your opinion wasn't asked.

EMILIANO. You're old enough to make your decision. But I warn you — *(Marina doesn't know what to do. She is confused by the whole situation.)*

KARIM. *(To Marina.)* You can leave with me now and we can pick up your clothes later. *(Karim starts to exit.)*

PAQUITA. *(In a loud voice.)* And you got to deal with me.

KARIM. *(In a loud voice.)* Don't worry! I want the divorce papers as much as you do.

PAQUITA. Then Monday at the attorney's office!

KARIM. At the attorney's office on Monday, then! *(Karim exits.)*

PAQUITA. Let's go, Marina. Let's go inside. *(Paquita grabs her arm. Marina pulls away.)*

MARINA. No.

EMILIANO. *(To Marina.)* Why don't you go with her inside?

MARINA. No. I'm going to stay here with you. *(Karim enters.)*

KARIM. Let's go. *(He grabs her hand.)*

MARINA. Leave me alone.

KARIM. Let's go.

EMILIANO. Leave her alone, she said. *(Karim brings her close to him.)*

MARINA. Let go of me —! *(Marina pulls away from him. Silence. Karim walks to another part of the terrace. He is like a lost animal.)*

KARIM. I know you're going to change your mind. *(Karim paces back and forth.)* I'll wait for you. *(Karim starts to exit.)*

EMILIANO. Didn't you hear what she said?

KARIM. *(To Emiliano.)* I'll be outside.

EMILIANO. Go with Paquita inside the house.

PAQUITA. Let's go. *(Paquita and Marina exit running. Emiliano takes the gun and exits. Lorca observes Emiliano and Karim from a distance.)*

LORCA. Now they are talking. They are pacing. They are struggling for the gun. They are shouting at each other but they don't hear anything. *(Shakes his head.)* They can only see what both of their eyes see, which is nothing but death. And they don't know that the killer and the one who gets killed have one thing in common, and that is to remember the same memory of the bullet. Except, the one who dies will remember in reverse, and the one who kills will remember towards the future. — That's it. I'll take the bullet. I'll take it. *(There is a gunshot. A second gunshot. Lorca is bathed in a surreal light.)* It only lasts a few seconds, doesn't it? Then suddenly a gush of moments, brief, evaporating ... one after another ... everything that your eyes got to see ... sounds ... the mud ... voices ... shots ... guards ... a car driving ... and before that, a cell ... and before that, questions, But what crime have I committed? Shut up, *maricón* ... faggot ... But what crime have I committed? I said shut up, you communist ... Then a punch ... A slap ... A kick in the belly ... And then the moon ... hope ... only one hope ... a note ... I'm writing a note to my father ... Dear Papá ... Please give the bearer of this note 1,000 pesetas to get me out of this place ... this hell ... And before that, the arrest ... And before ... And before ... *(Emiliano enters and the lights are back to normal. Emiliano's heart is beating very fast and he's out of breath.)*

EMILIANO. Am I dead? Am I dead now, Federico?

LORCA. No. You're not dead.

EMILIANO. But the shots ... The shots.

LORCA. If you were dead you'd be seeing moments of your life falling like an avalanche.

EMILIANO. But there were shots ...

LORCA. Are you bleeding, Emiliano?

EMILIANO. No, but the shots ...

LORCA. Are you bleeding?

EMILIANO. No ... no ... I'm not bleeding.

LORCA. Then nothing happened. Nothing happened. The boy missed.

EMILIANO. And were you here to take me away? Is that why you were here then?

LORCA. I don't know, my friend. One should never go before one's time. Trust me.

MARINA. *(Offstage.)* Papá!

LORCA. Straighten your clothes, *hombre.* Your family is coming. They're probably worried about you. *(Marina enters running.)*

MARINA. Papá! Are you all right? *(Silence. Emiliano's eyes are fixed on Lorca.)*

EMILIANO. Nothing happened.

MARINA. But we heard shots!

EMILIANO. There were shots, but nothing has happened. I'm here, am alive and I don't have any blood on my shirt. *(Marina looks at her father with certain compassion. There are tears in her eyes.*

Emiliano looks at her. There is distance and silence between them.
Emiliano picks up a nest from the floor. Paquita does the same. Marina
picks up the bundle that contains all the perfumes.)
MARINA. Is he gone?
EMILIANO. I don't know.
MARINA. He left all his perfumes behind.
PAQUITA. He'll come back for them.
EMILIANO. It's better if he doesn't.
MARINA. You're right. It's better if he doesn't.
PAQUITA. Let's cheer up, *hombre*. Nothing has happened here!
Nothing happened to you, nothing happened to Marina. Let's pick
up this place. Look at this light. *(She starts organizing the place.)*
When I heard those shots I remembered my days at the bullfights
when I was engaged to the toreador Amado Tenerife. He always
reserved a seat for me on the third row because he used to say that
I brought him good luck. Imagine me in a corrida, when I'm the
kind that faints at the sight of blood. I always had to carry a little
bottle of spirits in my purse, just in case I felt the fainting coming.
And every time Amado Tenerife used to stick a banderilla into the
neck of a bull, I had to take out my little bottle and take a sniff. It
used to make my heart race like a horse, and my face would get all
red. And between all the excitement at the bullfights and my little
bottle of spirits I suspect something happened to my heart, because
sometimes it feels … *(Touches her chest.)*
EMILIANO. Do you feel pain?
PAQUITA. Always around this time my heart races a little.
MARINA. That happens to all of us.
EMILIANO. Yes.
MARINA. How can I make it up to you, Papá?
EMILIANO. Make up what?
MARINA. All this. Everything that's happened since I got here.
EMILIANO. Just be who you are. Just be my daughter.
MARINA. I haven't done a good job at being that. I think I have
to learn to be a daughter all over again. *(Karim enters.)*
KARIM. Emiliano.
LORCA. Let him come back. Let him stay. — Tonight you will go
to bed companionless and perhaps discontent at the violence of
life, and when sleep comes, you will unwind yourself like the string
of a kite in the air, then you'll feel the weightlessness of your
human soul and realize that the sadness in your being when meas-
ured against the weight of world might seem very little. *(Emiliano*

walks to Karim and takes the gun from him.)
EMILIANO.   Let's clean up this place. *(Music begins to play. The family begins to put things back in their place.)*
LORCA.   No deaths reported today at five o'clock in the afternoon. No. No deaths. Only a father, a daughter and a young man playing marbles with their hearts, and a woman crying because she ran out of tears. As for me, I'm still here walking under the olive trees, and as I while away the time I memorize my life like an actor in a play, just in case I get to be in someone else's dream. After all, the living depend on our stories, and every night we must lend them our eyes and show them the little stream of blood that still flows from our wounds. *(Lorca **unbuttons** his vest and reveals two bullet holes. The lights begin to fade.)*

End of Play

PROPERTY LIST

Espadrilles
Birdcage
Bird's nests
Cloth
Cell phone
Paints
Canvas, paintbrushes, rag
Box of hats
Rifle
Bottles of oils
Arabesque cloth
Dropper
Towel
Rugs, carpet beater
Bottle of wine
Sketchpad, pencil
Paper
Cigarette, lighter
Boom box
Long silk scarf
Glass of milk
Sunglasses
Broken objects on wheeled platform
Tablecloth with sausages, wine, bread, fruit, napkins, etc.
Moon on a leash
Firewood
Hand puppet

SOUND EFFECTS

Bells
Flamenco music
Gunshot
Moroccan music
Techno music
Music
Fado music
Gunshots

NEW PLAYS

★ **THE EXONERATED by Jessica Blank and Erik Jensen.** Six interwoven stories paint a picture of an American criminal justice system gone horribly wrong and six brave souls who persevered to survive it. "The #1 play of the year...intense and deeply affecting..." *–NY Times.* "Riveting. Simple, honest storytelling that demands reflection." *–A.P.* "Artful and moving...pays tribute to the resilience of human hearts and minds." *–Variety.* "Stark...riveting...cunningly orchestrated." *–The New Yorker.* "Hard-hitting, powerful, and socially relevant." *–Hollywood Reporter.* [7M, 3W] ISBN: 0-8222-1946-8

★ **STRING FEVER by Jacquelyn Reingold.** Lily juggles the big issues: turning forty, artificial insemination and the elusive scientific Theory of Everything in this Off-Broadway comedy hit. "Applies the elusive rules of string theory to the conundrums of one woman's love life. Think *Sex and the City* meets *Copenhagen*." *–NY Times.* "A funny offbeat and touching look at relationships...an appealing romantic comedy populated by oddball characters." *–NY Daily News.* "Where kooky, zany, and madcap meet...whimsically winsome." *–NY Magazine.* "STRING FEVER will have audience members happily stringing along." *–TheaterMania.com.* "Reingold's language is surprising, inventive, and unique." *–nytheatre.com.* "...[a] whimsical comic voice." *–Time Out.* [3M, 3W (doubling)] ISBN: 0-8222-1952-2

★ **DEBBIE DOES DALLAS adapted by Erica Schmidt, composed by Andrew Sherman, conceived by Susan L. Schwartz.** A modern morality tale told as a comic musical of tragic proportions as the classic film is brought to the stage. "A scream! A saucy, tongue-in-cheek romp." *–The New Yorker.* "Hilarious! DEBBIE manages to have it all: beauty, brains and a great sense of humor!" *–Time Out.* "Shamelessly silly, shrewdly self-aware and proud of being naughty. Great fun!" *–NY Times.* "Racy and raucous, a lighthearted, fast-paced thoroughly engaging and hilarious send-up." *–NY Daily News.* [3M, 5W] ISBN: 0-8222-1955-7

★ **THE MYSTERY PLAYS by Roberto Aguirre-Sacasa.** Two interrelated one acts, loosely based on the tradition of the medieval mystery plays. "... stylish, spine-tingling...Mr. Aguirre-Sacasa uses standard tricks of horror stories, borrowing liberally from masters like Kafka, Lovecraft, Hitchcock...But his mastery of the genre is his own...irresistible." *–NY Times.* "Undaunted by the special-effects limitations of theatre, playwright and *Marvel* comic-book writer Roberto Aguirre-Sacasa maps out some creepy twilight zones in THE MYSTERY PLAYS, an engaging, related pair of one acts...The theatre may rarely deliver shocks equivalent to, say, *Dawn of the Dead*, but Aguirre-Sacasa's work is fine compensation." *–Time Out.* [4M, 2W] ISBN: 0-8222-2038-5

★ **THE JOURNALS OF MIHAIL SEBASTIAN by David Auburn.** This epic one-man play spans eight tumultuous years and opens a uniquely personal window on the Romanian Holocaust and the Second World War. "Powerful." *–NY Times.* "[THE JOURNALS OF MIHAIL SEBASTIAN] allows us to glimpse the idiosyncratic effects of that awful history on one intelligent, pragmatic, recognizably real man..." *–NY Newsday.* [3M, 5W] ISBN: 0-8222-2006-7

★ **LIVING OUT by Lisa Loomer.** The story of the complicated relationship between a Salvadoran nanny and the Anglo lawyer she works for. "A stellar new play. Searingly funny." *–The New Yorker.* "Both generous and merciless, equally enjoyable and disturbing." *–NY Newsday.* "A bitingly funny new comedy. The plight of working mothers is explored from two pointedly contrasting perspectives in this sympathetic, sensitive new play." *–Variety.* [2M, 6W] ISBN: 0-8222-1994-8

DRAMATISTS PLAY SERVICE, INC.
440 Park Avenue South, New York, NY 10016   212-683-8960   Fax 212-213-1539
postmaster@dramatists.com   www.dramatists.com

NEW PLAYS

★ **MATCH by Stephen Belber.** Mike and Lisa Davis interview a dancer and choreographer about his life, but it is soon evident that their agenda will either ruin or inspire them—and definitely change their lives forever. "Prolific laughs and ear-to-ear smiles." *–NY Magazine.* "Uproariously funny, deeply moving, enthralling theater. Stephen Belber's MATCH has great beauty and tenderness, and abounds in wit." *–NY Daily News.* "Three and a half out of four stars." *–USA Today.* "A theatrical steeplechase that leads straight from outrageous bitchery to unadorned, heartfelt emotion." *–Wall Street Journal.* [2M, 1W] ISBN: 0-8222-2020-2

★ **HANK WILLIAMS: LOST HIGHWAY by Randal Myler and Mark Harelik.** The story of the beloved and volatile country-music legend Hank Williams, featuring twenty-five of his most unforgettable songs. "[LOST HIGHWAY has] the exhilarating feeling of Williams on stage in a particular place on a particular night…serves up classic country with the edges raw and the energy hot…By the end of the play, you've traveled on a profound emotional journey: LOST HIGHWAY transports its audience and communicates the inspiring message of the beauty and richness of Williams' songs…forceful, clear-eyed, moving, impressive." *–Rolling Stone.* "…honors a very particular musical talent with care and energy… smart, sweet, poignant." *–NY Times.* [7M, 3W] ISBN: 0-8222-1985-9

★ **THE STORY by Tracey Scott Wilson.** An ambitious black newspaper reporter goes against her editor to investigate a murder and finds the *best* story…but at what cost? "A singular new voice…deeply emotional, deeply intellectual, and deeply musical…" *–The New Yorker.* "…a conscientious and absorbing new drama…" *–NY Times.* "…a riveting, tough-minded drama about race, reporting and the truth…" *–A.P.* "… a stylish, attention-holding script that ends on a chilling note that will leave viewers with much to talk about." *–Curtain Up.* [2M, 7W (doubling, flexible casting)] ISBN: 0-8222-1998-0

★ **OUR LADY OF 121st STREET by Stephen Adly Guirgis.** The body of Sister Rose, beloved Harlem nun, has been stolen, reuniting a group of life-challenged childhood friends who square off as they wait for her return. "A scorching and dark new comedy… Mr. Guirgis has one of the finest imaginations for dialogue to come along in years." *–NY Times.* "Stephen Guirgis may be the best playwright in America under forty." *–NY Magazine.* [8M, 4W] ISBN: 0-8222-1965-4

★ **HOLLYWOOD ARMS by Carrie Hamilton and Carol Burnett.** The coming-of-age story of a dreamer who manages to escape her bleak life and follow her romantic ambitions to stardom. Based on Carol Burnett's bestselling autobiography, *One More Time.* "…pure theatre and pure entertainment…" *–Talkin' Broadway.* "…a warm, fuzzy evening of theatre." *–BrodwayBeat.com.* "…chuckles and smiles of recognition or surprise flow naturally…a remarkable slice of life." *–TheatreScene.net.* [5M, 5W, 1 girl] ISBN: 0-8222-1959-X

★ **INVENTING VAN GOGH by Steven Dietz.** A haunting and hallucinatory drama about the making of art, the obsession to create and the fine line that separates truth from myth. "Like a van Gogh painting, Dietz's story is a gorgeous example of excess—one that remakes reality with broad, well-chosen brush strokes. At evening's end, we're left with the author's resounding opinions on art and artifice, and provoked by his constant query into which is greater: van Gogh's art or his violent myth." *–Phoenix New Times.* "Dietz's writing is never simple. It is always brilliant. Shaded, compressed, direct, lucid—he frames his subject with a remarkable understanding of painting as a physical experience." *–Tucson Citizen.* [4M, 1W] ISBN: 0-8222-1954-9

DRAMATISTS PLAY SERVICE, INC.
440 Park Avenue South, New York, NY 10016 212-683-8960 Fax 212-213-1539
postmaster@dramatists.com   www.dramatists.com

NEW PLAYS

★ **INTIMATE APPAREL by Lynn Nottage.** The moving and lyrical story of a turn-of-the-century black seamstress whose gifted hands and sewing machine are the tools she uses to fashion her dreams from the whole cloth of her life's experiences. "...Nottage's play has a delicacy and eloquence that seem absolutely right for the time she is depicting..." –*NY Daily News.* "...thoughtful, affecting...The play offers poignant commentary on an era when the cut and color of one's dress—and of course, skin—determined whom one could and could not marry, sleep with, even talk to in public." –*Variety.* [2M, 4W] ISBN: 0-8222-2009-1

★ **BROOKLYN BOY by Donald Margulies.** A witty and insightful look at what happens to a writer when his novel hits the bestseller list. "The characters are beautifully drawn, the dialogue sparkles..." –*nytheatre.com.* "Few playwrights have the mastery to smartly investigate so much through a laugh-out-loud comedy that combines the vintage subject matter of successful writer-returning-to-ethnic-roots with the familiar mid-life crisis." –*Show Business Weekly.* [4M, 3W] ISBN: 0-8222-2074-1

★ **CROWNS by Regina Taylor.** Hats become a springboard for an exploration of black history and identity in this celebratory musical play. "Taylor pulls off a Hat Trick: She scores thrice, turning CROWNS into an artful amalgamation of oral history, fashion show, and musical theater..." –*TheatreMania.com.* "...wholly theatrical...Ms. Taylor has created a show that seems to arise out of spontaneous combustion, as if a bevy of department-store customers simultaneously decided to stage a revival meeting in the changing room." –*NY Times.* [1M, 6W (2 musicians)] ISBN: 0-8222-1963-8

★ **EXITS AND ENTRANCES by Athol Fugard.** The story of a relationship between a young playwright on the threshold of his career and an aging actor who has reached the end of his. "[Fugard] can say more with a single line than most playwrights convey in an entire script...Paraphrasing the title, it's safe to say this drama, making its memorable entrance into our consciousness, is unlikely to exit as long as a theater exists for exceptional work." –*Variety.* "A thought-provoking, elegant and engrossing new play..." –*Hollywood Reporter.* [2M] ISBN: 0-8222-2041-5

★ **BUG by Tracy Letts.** A thriller featuring a pair of star-crossed lovers in an Oklahoma City motel facing a bug invasion, paranoia, conspiracy theories and twisted psychological motives. "...obscenely exciting...top-flight craftsmanship. Buckle up and brace yourself..." –*NY Times.* "...[a] thoroughly outrageous and thoroughly entertaining play...the possibility of enemies, real and imagined, to squash has never been more theatrical." –*A.P.* [3M, 2W] ISBN: 0-8222-2016-4

★ **THOM PAIN (BASED ON NOTHING) by Will Eno.** An ordinary man muses on childhood, yearning, disappointment and loss, as he draws the audience into his last-ditch plea for empathy and enlightenment. "It's one of those treasured nights in the theater—treasured nights anywhere, for that matter—that can leave you both breathless with exhilaration and...in a puddle of tears." –*NY Times.* "Eno's words...are familiar, but proffered in a way that is constantly contradictory to our expectations. Beckett is certainly among his literary ancestors." –*nytheatre.com.* [1M] ISBN: 0-8222-2076-8

★ **THE LONG CHRISTMAS RIDE HOME by Paula Vogel.** Past, present and future collide on a snowy Christmas Eve for a troubled family of five. "...[a] lovely and hauntingly original family drama...a work that breathes so much life into the theater." –*Time Out.* "...[a] delicate visual feast..." –*NY Times.* "...brutal and lovely...the overall effect is magical." –*NY Newsday.* [3M, 3W] ISBN: 0-8222-2003-2

DRAMATISTS PLAY SERVICE, INC.
440 Park Avenue South, New York, NY 10016 212-683-8960 Fax 212-213-1539
postmaster@dramatists.com www.dramatists.com